FATHER OF NOISE

ANTHONY MCCANN

FENCEbooks

Cover photograph:

8.8.88 by Tomas Ruller.
Courtesy Ronald Feldman Fine Arts,
New York.

Published in the United States by

Fence Books
14 Fifth Avenue, #1A
New York, NY 10011
www.fencebooks.com

Saturnalia Books
122 Hartswick Ave.
State College, PA 16803
www.saturnaliabooks.com

Book design by

Saturnalia Books

Fence Books is distributed by

University Press of New England
www.upne.com

Library of Congress Cataloguing in Publication Data
McCann, Anthony
Father of Noise / Anthony McCann

Library of Congress Control Number: 2003101447

ISBN 0-9713189-6-4

FIRST EDITION

Printed in Canada

The author wishes to acknowledge, thank and tease his father for his support and critique of
this work and for his endless, at times unprovoked, recitations of Shakespeare, Dickinson and
Yeats. The author would also like to acknowledge and formally thank all his fantastic friends
for the support, encouragement, and good times without which this book would have been
impossible. Thanks to Rebecca Wolff, Henry Israeli, Joanna Goodman and everyone at
Fence/Saturnalia. Special thanks to Joanna for being such an attentive reader and helpful
editor. Big thanks too to Kerry Keys and everyone associated with Pine Press in Vilnius.
The author also needs to express his eternal gratitude to Sam Witt, Matt Rohrer and Mark Allen
for their enthusiasm for and efforts on behalf of this work. Extra eternal gratitude goes to Karen
McCann, Ed and Sarah Denison, Laura McCann and Kevin Jones. Lastly the author must thank
Ellen Sharp for the last eleven years. This book is for her and for the rest of the family.

The author also wishes to thank the editors of the magazines in which some of these poems
first appeared, sometimes in different form: *Fine Madness*, *Fence*, *Conduit*, *Lit*, *Canary River
Review*, *Prairie Schooner*, *Teacup*, and *Trepan*.

Table of Contents

IN PRAISE OF REASON

Y muere un sentimiento antiguo/degenerado en seso.

—Cesár Vallejo

Empire State

Father of Noise Ceremony

It was the end of fingerprints, fingerprints
As we knew them.
Is what the ceremony said. It said
It was impersonating us.
So began the season of forgetting.
All was painted blue:
The clouds, the space between the clouds.
Our cities went, we watched them go, becoming sky.
Who is The Father of Noise?
Is what the voices said.
It was the death of romance, romance
As we knew him.
With his horse dancers, with his hundred mouths.
Who is the Father of Anything?
Is what the dancers say, they said
We were impersonating them.
And blowing air out through their hose.
But at the end of something, something
Had finally happened.
It's how the moaning started.
And now we are its mouth.
Our bodies go, we watch them go, becoming land.
These are not my fingers, we say.
And we put our faces on our pillows and drown.

Skywalker Ranch

I was struggling to embrace the new technology
when quite on accident I drained the harbor, dredged the locks,
and devastated the local economy now finding myself
still trying to yoke this motor, runaway outboard
in a burrowing fury.
O my heart, manic mudskipper, surging in mud.
Writing these lines I am overcome with fatigue and despair as if
the temperature had risen suddenly and I,
inner pioneer and amateur pharmacologist, were sweating
true bricks!
I give up, get off my knees, take off my lifejacket.
Because no one lives here anymore, except security
and the gardeners. I am the world's last actor,
I have to inspect the "winery." Add some more dust
to the bottles, peel more paint from the barn,
sodomize the ingrates. Do you have a raygun
or perhaps a stick of commemorative gum? I need to pretend
that I am under attack from the air.

Jack

Jack, which is not his real name, was concerned about the progress of his recovery. The rest of us couldn't understand because we were immigrants, not entirely legal, and besides we stood outside the doors of that facility exporting rain and comparing rocks. Jack is a Large American Man of a Typical Brand. He is like a Helicopter or he is like an Amphibious Assault Vehicle. His entire body is covered in hair: his arms his hands with which he is always touching me. Jack's eyes are small and dry which is surprising considering the enormity and moisture of his apparent need. (What Jack hopes to recover I do not understand.) He is always looking me in the eyes with those eyes or, if not, he is always looking away as if toward the mountains which do not exist in this country. The land here is scarred and flat and faintly evil and I still cannot accurately pronounce its name. (No one here can pronounce my name so I too am called Jack.)

Immigrant Theory

As America eats chalk and waits for the bus
I am waiting right here to get in
I'm standing here next to my bike
I'm assessing the air and the rubber
My hands are a greased up disaster
My ideas are all covered in sperm
Because America's an idea about milk
Conceived in a bright sweet machine
And I'm waiting right here to go up
Into a purer perfection of Brooklyn
In my 40 dollar shoes
In my 40 dollar shirt
I have some ideas about shoes
Everything else gets unsaid

Experience

A creeping silence follows our party as the day fades and still we are working our way inland, to the splash and groan of our oars. Right now I am watching some sort of spiny looking water mammal, with doggish eyes, slurching alongside our craft. It disappears in the water, the water stained a heavy blue with the encroaching dusk, reemerging suddenly now with a deep plop. I attempt to describe it here for the journal I will publish upon returning to the angry and colorless city of my birth. *It is shapeless, and yet its meat seems firm, with eyes unlike any creature, spaced wide apart and possessed of a certain intelligence, though its appearance be monstrous.* And I am tempted and it is then that I make the mistake of an untrained adventurer touching the forbidden surface of that country with my still tender, unprotected, palm.

Peacekeeper and The War of Things

I saw 4 birds in el trayecto.
Each one smaller onto death.
Each an object oozing twine.
Leaking twigs and code.
Little alphabets of breath.
Cake in the distance,
a dusted hill...
Which is what they say
in love as in war.
Such gentle people
with *real* hands.
Never seen such
real hands.
Let's cross ourselves
against the thought of
all their bodies
oozing life.
Let's touch the livid woods.
The polished counted stars.
And Dawn: The Perfect Wound
with its alphabet of cops
digging in the pants
with sticks, the pockets
spilling code...

Empire State

A bright disturbance
Drags us

Further north into

Deepest Indian Country

Fresh Smoke over

Fresh Snow
(The snow fell all night

on their camp in the swamp)
Now I will describe

This train with my body

•

The river cuts deeper
Into the soft rock and foam

Beneath my dead skin
My true skin was burning

My heart is a leathery stick

I'm in the army now
Surfing toward Peekskill

To score

•

After the massacre
We pitched our tents

Right here

In the blood-slick snow
A bright storm

On the surface

Of a mind: And I am stricken

With nostalgia
For the New World

Throughout the story
These same lines are repeated

My heart is a leathery stick

Jumping from Platform
Is Illegal

And Dangerous

•

I wanted to worship
This world with my mouth

Fresh steam rolling

Over the frosted hills

The infrastructure singing
The infrastructure song

Bon Soir, I say,
To the ducks

In Dutch

The muskrat chunneling
In the wintry isles

O liquor I am stricken
With a bloomed nostalgia

In the foreground: an irreversible power

The Action

the valley gives off steam
a car with enigmatic plates
slices through the afternoon
the visitors have entered the landscape
behind the tree
something breathes
and then nothing happens
this is god's country
someone whispers
approaching from the air

Starkweather

The land that crunches underfoot. The frozen stalk.

As if there weren't no one left in the world.

Because Nebraska is a headache. (The skin is stretched thin

across the throbbing skull, the veins show.)

The viaduct sits up over the town and the town is dead.

The milky way is stretched thin over frozen Nebraska, over the

eviscerated animals.

I will now describe the building
in which he lived.

•

I will now describe the building
in which he lived.

A sprawling structure of units.

•

The biography is full of details.
The land crunches underfoot.

These details attach themselves
to the surface of Nebraska.

The silence after domestic violence.

The animal crunches underfoot

spewing thin, dead stars.

•

This is a poem called Nebraska.

Nebraska is full of details.

The clothesline, the iced broom, the wounded backs

of cars on blocks, poking up out of the frozen stalks

that crank and crack in the amplified wind under

Thin, dead stars.

•

This is a poem called Nebraska.

A sprawling structure of units.

•

The biography is full of details.

Highway machines and hardhearted men.

Highway machines and hardhearted men.

The scent of blood like rust.

The frozen land, the highway shapes.

The wounded broom.

All of it evidence.

•

I will people Nebraska with tight lips and cold.

With the silence of kitchens at night following the domestic violence.

The neon sign that does not blink.

The faucet that does not drip.

•

Because Nebraska is a headache.
Because the skin is stretched thin.
Because the land is froze and flat.
I comb my hair and I grease it back.

Patriot's Day

There are citizenship issues before dawn.
The air hangs without taste and through it
all planes are poured.
When the axe descends nothing sounds.
Sun smashes on the traps
and the day is caught by its tufted foot.
This space gets all rezoned in light.
The neighborhood resigns—
but we'll come crawling back
through all this heat
without our names,
unreleased, to watch these fields burn.

Drug War

'Twas first morning of the war:
usual riot of avarian light
and the forest scribbled down, rattling the dirt
and as we bird-watched I exclaimed
—citizens, this is how to lick the dust,
and light candles near to death—
while out comes oil from the guts
which is where the coke went down
down some eyeway in the earth and
with all forest on no sides
we didn't know what we could eat.
So here's a camera you can smoke
while we light someone in mud
where we burn fingers on his face
till he's so high he couldn't speak

All About My Monkey

He is an object and he eats the dusk.
I call him Revolution.
In the desert he was the absence of dessert.
Wind ruffled his nits under
darkness, clear darkness with two moons.
When the mountain came he barked.
(When Coach came he howled.)
He has four limbs but two knees—
they lick glass and dissolve thirst.
Just the speed of his teeth
returns appropriated thoughts.
These are hips and other bones.
We view them under water with special lights.
They are objects that we trust—
like coins and blood.
Near this place where we are standing
he captured me and made me clear.
So unleashed I walk among you.
It's all a joke my monkey made
about some office he declined.
Mewling in the dark
for plastic, fumbling with his hands,
he offers me my rights.
What are these rights?
I met him on a bicycle
tooling through this park.
We are objects where we meet the sky

to the smell of horse and burning cars—
when we finish in this place
it's sure to end in tears.

Elegy

And as my own hands reappear like those of ill relations
on the couch suddenly there without intention
or malice.
And as the light breaks itself against my face
I say: "Uncle." I say: "If I could only touch your face."
"Face of the world not its face." "You."
If I could speak this
in your ear, the very ear of it, the other side.
If I could remove this bird from this train.
I want to give you that place which is yours.
Stumbling a little like this now, nose down, hands on my ears
screaming "my ears" past this and then that
dark green truck. I think:
"Sanitation." I think:
"My ears you assholes." I am ranting
or I am groveling, it is one or the other
with our imaginary race. Words come because we are built from noise.
But when I entered the kitchen today I smelled you
and I went like this
over the graves, over the streets of sirens and music
like sirens in the street.
I found a stain and I called it "Here."
I called it
"Where it happens." Where I hide my face
one face inside, where I break this light in mirror time.
And I pressed myself against it, pretending all of this.

Confessions

My Relationship with Jesus

I am looking at the sky which is blue and empty and thinking of his lips which are closed and dry. Or standing in front of students with my mouth open like this I am thinking about him, in a ratty towel, saying nothing on the phone. Watching TV and smoking one endless cigarette. He doesn't even cough. It enrages me. I hold it in. I can't stop coughing. I swear it's because of him and the emotional duress his depression and distance cause me that I develop certain unpleasant sores about the lip and in my oral cavity. Inside my mouth. It makes me feel ugly. "It makes me feel ugly," I say. I say, "Kiss me." He changes the channel. He puts on a shirt. It's a green shirt, a sort of lime-green shirt. I like that shirt. I ask him if he likes my body.

Confessions

beginnings

Before money and California;
before the state of Massachusetts
there was a river and it had a name.
Another mossy indian-sounding name.
Woodlands Indian.
There was a river and it loved the land.
The land was rich with whatever land
is rich with, minerals and vitamins I guess.
But then it was scraped away, into the river,
with imported tools, by incompetent invaders
who were cruel and stupid
and filled the land with package stores
and the towns grew and grew around them.
And into this land I was born.
Or so it is said. All I want to tell here Lord
is that I do not know where I really came from
when I was born into this life.
But I was content to suck.
And so I grew to the next stage.

adolescence

I could call this a revolt.
This next stage.
I don't remember
when it started.
I could call it Woburn.
Or I could call it Braintree.
What I remember is that boredom,
its shape. I have driven
that car. But this one time
I was in love—this was before California.
This was after Panama
but before the Gulf.
I had a brand new pair
of excellent boots and
I drove my car fast
along the river's curves.
Forgive me Lord, I didn't know
what I was really like.

confession

There was a young woman from another state who in my
youth I mistreated. We said angry and sappy and stupid
things as youths will do because we thought we understood
our tongue. There are no photographs of us. But take it that
she was an unattractive girl and I was an unattractive boy.
Together we did unattractive things. Until then I had imag-
ined that I was kind; a somehow wounded young man.
I don't remember what actors I admired. But then I discov-
ered arrogance and cruelty and silence in particular and she
went back to her boyfriend a small and truly kind boy who
played the acoustic guitar. I went and stood at the edge of
a frozen parking lot on the edge of that city where the city
gives way and the liquor gives way to an empty Taco Time
and the death of all enthusiasm. I had some other friends
with me, they were asleep in the car and, Lord, I thought
they all looked retarded.

received wisdom

Once there was a boy
who wouldn't look up
or he wouldn't look down
I can't remember
and in his mouth he held
a precious stone
He was a stupid boy
The End
Or once there was a boy

who lived all alone in the world
except for his friend
Mr. Egg
And he got what he deserved

and the next stage

And the next stage
is California.

california

The coast was covered in fog
as I came up over
the ridge in our car
listening to a sad
and triumphant
California song.
I was some kind
of superstar, pissing
in the parking lot
over the Pacific
near the RV's.
What else
can I say?
I came here
searching for you,
through the
interior, dry like a mouth.

Subsisting on bagels
and dope.
And I drove on
into the city, where I went amongst them.
I examined their flesh
and found it to be weak.
Pushed to a certain wall,
my arms and legs
bent to their pleasure,
I expired at dawn.
Giving up the ghost, this body and breath, up
into the cruel blue air.
Beginning again, naked and curled
in a stranger's bed.

Walk and Missive

Last night was fetish night
at the Lava Lounge. All the foreigners were lining up
for hygienic and professional abuse.
We are all engaged in this lugubrious parody of pleasure
because we
are Phony Balonies. (I am looking
for a real commitment.)
Meanwhile, here, back in the neighborhood
the local children are dragging the chicken.
This involves a tricycle, a length of pink ribbon,
and one four-year-old with all the enthusiasm of the world
required to counter the pure reluctance of chicken.
Around and around the "block" they go.
Its is 1:30 on a Sunday afternoon and I am amazed.
Please, picture me like this, have this
picture of me, a little blurry in the face
but the decal is distinct.
I have enough cash in my pocket
for once. I touch it and imagine it transformed
into cold beer and sandwiches.
The river is, of course, poisonous.
Now I pass two men in white, practicing
tae kwon do, as speechless and breathy as breeze
in semi-professional grass.
Is it freedom to be alive and not thinking
about not thinking about it?
I pass them thinking
what else I don't remember.

Seoul, September '97

Breathing

I put my best face forward
as if it were a face
bobbing like a hologram
over the ocean of my uniform.
As if it were a face.
Not so much self-inflated mush.
I try not to think
about my underpants.
Underpants are a part
of my uniform.
The invisible part.
Not thinking about them
takes up a great deal of time.
It is important to take up time,
to stay busy.
It says so in the manual.
Where is that manual?
It's right here,
in front of my face.
I mistook it
for my ears.
It's that powerful.
It'll take your ears right off.
Like falling down the stairs.
Like Mental Hospitals,
cheap blonde ones.
I got cut off once
but that's not important.
What is important

is to stay positive,
to meet people
and join their organizations.
It is important to practice
my martial arts.
"Pffft." is the sound
of my karate kick
in empty space.
"Pffft."
There we go.
I said it again.
That was refreshing.
Like air.
Air is refreshing.
It is important.
It is cardiovascular.
Babies need it.
Traffic needs it.
Right in the arteries.
I'll tell you a secret.
I invented it.
With my mouth
I imitate it.
Like telephones ringing,
like a penis.
It's an imitation.
I do it with my mouth.
I make a space.
I call it breathing.

The Young Investigators

Near the marsh we find a shoe signifying
Aunt Cindy. A truck goes by, rattling our spines. Signifying a chill
up the spine. We thought such traffic
had been prohibited. Day two:
Grandmother has new evidence of us in the photo album,
next to the reeds, the marsh, the impossibility of Georgia on our mind.
We go down to the ocean with salt on our hands and weep. Who was Cindy?
Who bombed the Plain of Jars?
We don't want to return to the hotel, to the future,
pre-eulogized, well-toasted: Grandfather bobbing
in his birthday like a cork.
I'm sitting at this table with my mouth open. Day three:
Once real Rockefellers
roamed these gazebos. We are photographed next to their photographs, sitting
in their chairs. Eating with their forks.
It's part of the package. *Pheasant Hunting, Croquet*
is the first song on our new album. That very night: In the lounge,
Robert Mitchum from Out of the Past.
His heart, sturdy Packard, mired in mud. Day four:
Florida approaching, with humility and stealth.
In the cool and empty garage: American Music.

American Experience

1.

I am trying to have an experience here
in the front yard (I've walked around the house)
in this square of dead grass
with all this shit
like the dead tree and its two
stumpy arms outstretched and the insects
which are very dead and real.
Here under the sky which is genuine
and greasy. A little low and green today
as if it's been touched with mold.
And I am on a lot of drugs which you should know
before you approach me.
Because I am trying to have an experience.
I am truly fucked up here in
the front yard of my house with
the tree and the dying grass and the other miscellaneous
plant life. And what was it I was waiting for here
in middle of the goddamned afternoon?
I was waiting for the airplane to pass
to come sliding in over the trees its
glittering belly exposed
obscene and beautiful. Like you could touch it
and it would be
cold and dry and surprising.
And I was trying to have an experience

because that was an experience I could have
with the drugs and machinery
in this low-rent district that borders the airport.
Because my body is primed for disaster.

2.

Next door there is the house
with the Rottweilers
and behind me our house
with its dead window and the awkward silence
which is why I am out here in the lawn
looking for the good times.
It's a bestial day in the neighborhood.
The man with the Rottweilers, my neighbor
to the right, he is a fence.
And when we have shook hands I have
actually succeeded
in having an experience. I felt
like an American. I swear
my muscle acquires more tone
and my voice
drops an octave and I feel
excellent and cynical about this weather
and the whole damn world
when I talk to this man
who is a genuine successful criminal
with a house
and a big TV and three dogs in this neighborhood.
Whereas I am only an amateur
with a taste for disaster.

3.

And I am trying to have an experience here
in the front yard with the
struggling grass and the dogs
and the sky which is greasy
and low. Here with the dead tree
and its comical stumps I am trying
to concentrate. To hit the right note
with my body and these chemicals
as the airplane comes cruising in from the west side
sliding like a giant rock song across the surface
of this neighborhood. I'm out here
with the plants and the houses
and all the other shit
making ready for the noise
that will cause my body to vibrate
into a realignment. And I'm like waiting
for this big and excellent disaster.

American Summertime Prayer

O Lord let me be shallow and good looking and not just
a little drunk and sort of naked in your dream
that feels like blue fingers on my skin here
on the lakefront as the last light is wrung from your sky.
Is this the last year before the war?
Let me love these strangers then, these
forlorn and furious recreators. Can I please?
They are so weird. Let us all
have sex together with our mouths and the police.
Give us this day this dreadful street and its OK shrubs
and a house full of dope and booze and
give me a sly tongue and a body
agile and cruel. Let it be
like this. Brain kissed quiet, ear well tuned, mind
like a fresh carpet. The one I lay on
early this afternoon—heavy
in the voice of traffic. The world, the yard, tattooed with bugs.
Let it sizzle with sound. Let it cook. Let it be the summer
of tits and cocks and jumping off bridges
into still water heavy
with the shadows of trees. Let it be the season
of not contracting disease
of the blood or liver.
O Lord, here on Planet X
where I love my girl and bright mustache
and my name, which is Rick, and the wind
which pours over my body
and also my bicycle and my machine gun and all my other stuff,
let me be Lord, let me breathe.

Report From The Surface

1.

You do not understand but
I have been to the other side and
part of me is not here, here
in the parking lot, on this planet
with the parking meters like stray hairs.
The parking meters are my friends. Excuse me:
I would like to befriend the lonely things
but it does not stop it.
Stop me from eating them. Snapping their necks.
Crunching their heads. O.
Being here. On this planet
with the weird thing bubbling
just beneath the surface. And all that we can do
is to stand here
in our too-tight suits with the insignia.
All that we can do is to
touch the plants and smile, the little silver plants
that shiver. This is not OK.
But it does not stop me.
So you see that I am an unusual person
in the uniform of the starfleet.
That it is painful to move my neck like this.
That I am not happy.

2.

My heart is beating so fast I enter a kind of sleep.
Here in the window I drift
                    in the glamorous noise
of buses. O generous vehicles!...

(Am I hungry? I think that I might be hungry.)

Nice trees you have here on this planet,
Very Nice Trees.

Did I mention that I was hungry?

*

Most pleasant weather! Most admirable sky!
And yet I felt somehow it was terribly nearby
right there, just above my head and somehow
edible. Bland, crumbly, like a cracker.
Most breakable, like my face.

My heart is beating so fast I enter a kind of sleep.
I am a vague thing, with arms and legs.

Call me Visitor.

Here on this planet, this obscure planet with trees
and pleasant machinery (well lit and
most admirable), I am hardly here.

3.

O, to be here in the parking lot
on this planet, with the parking meters like spiteful hairs.
You do not understand.
I am all alone here. I am the entire away team.
On this delirious planet I say we
out of some need. As in
all that we can do.
As in all that we can do
is to touch
the too tight pants and smile.
The pants with the insignia. O.
It is painful to move my jaw like this.
Here on this planet where the tired thing moves
just beneath the surface
and I am vague and hungry.

My People

There we will be, you and I in the future,
in our apartment complexes
smoking cigarettes in our Teflon suits
while admiring ourselves. Outside the sky
is Teflon Blue, a new flavor and it is whizzing
with cheerful hovercraft.
The metropolis has been redesigned, reimagined,
with horns and secret compartments.
It's an excitable town, dense with fun.
If our Teflon suits seem tight it is because our bodies
are always changing.
It is to promote the so-called disco dancing.
Teflon hats stimulate the brain
making it a powerful sex organ.
We will say things to each other when we meet
in the skyway, in the future,
things like "Hello" and
"aren't you looking fraught and
brainy today underneath this sky
which is an intelligent shade
of Teflon."
Because we are pleasant creatures
with well-trained
and thoughtful appendages, because we are tender
and electronically sensitized, because
we weep regularly together and alone
ecstatically, because we weep sexually

in the trembling lobbies and moving sidewalks,
because we visit each other in these brilliant terminals
and touch hands and know each other's shame there is
no need for government, only these fantasies
we collect from ourselves
with the tiny and delightfully intrusive
transmitters in our little Teflon hats. We are
excellent space people in our
tight little pants. (The *others*
compare us to gazelles and giraffes—
we remain *their* children.)

Mayakovsky

At the party I remember my finger in your nose
                    strumming through the bodies on my way to the orange
bathroom where I piss
and feel tasty and obscene.

Absurd in the orange!

(It's delightful and obscene this living.)

Our bodies like the strange
        the pulsing mouths of strange

Electric Fish!

And were those your hands in my pants darling?
(Honestly dude, I don't remember.)

The whole evening was like this:

A cloud in the room not unlike smoke touching
every corner every plane

                        and we'll call it love.
Some sort of connective tissue.

epilogue —

and when I wake up in the morning in the living room
surrounded by your sleeping bodies
and I feel a little dark and ashamed

    and I feel a little like Jones at Jonestown

I wonder if you could all still possibly love me so
I leave this note
and sign it with an X.

Geek

Sucking the sick and yellow meat
from scrawny days and then:

"My toes"

              "Active as levers."

So violent bored and with it
this o so predictable desire
to break things——-

But with method.

One plate at a time.
Tick   Tock

The Whole Collection.

And then:

Maybe drool a bit.

Really, I'm down in the pits
feeling around in the dark for bones

words that snap like

"Turkeyneck."

And I'm in here like a box, breathing.

•

I walk around in circles
inside my tired routine

Behind unintended gestures
I watch

Ragged with chemicals
infected with meaning

always bored
and violently so

So I just go faster as if
on the other side of speed

were pleasure. And what a joke.
And I'm a joker—

Always about to "lose it"
on stage

So that
everyone in this room
is embarrassed for me.

●

O tell me comrades
why every dream of collectivity
organized inevitably
about me?

And doctor, please:
where from this mania
for linebreak and
for enigma?

Always waiting for the perfect silence
to inject something of interest
and win admirers.

Being Good (The Homeopath)

Today the rain kissed my pregnancy.
It was a slight Grand Slam
With tiny wings but
Mostly it was a kiss—
Which was a good idea
About myself
Forgiving Rain
Of all its thoughts.
Where my voice goes
I can't come back.
Riding through all this
Pigeon Noise was
Some kind of a
disease I cured
With Pigeon Noise
And bicycles.
I walk inside a speech
That I know is not my own.
Here on trains
I'll let you listen to my pores—Stop!
I'm feeling things like
Aluminum, like Seats.
It's not a game but
Like a sound
It is a thing that fails—
Like people and like trains.
I'm really small.

Where I'm standing now
Everything is closed.
I hear my face,
It never falls.

Bay Parkway and 86th

The pope looks like a painting of a pope as he
signs me into this as he
legislates me
to think. I am a creation of post-pope utility
called post-robot deficiency. I am reading *Newsweek*
in the world. The pope thinks
it is time for me to think. Suddenly
I am not catholic anymore.
Now I am post-rock
hysteria in the post-pharmaceutical fix.
What use is this fact today
on this day without air or with air so poured
through the cracks of today's
elevated rail? It's an inbound B train
that makes my body shake.
I've never been
outside this skin so now
I regret this place.
Sun so poured from overhead
where I go without a tongue to trade
for self. (Now I am post-ideological bliss
at the pre-futurist mass.)
Rumble This, Rumble That.
The world so touched in shapes of light
and news, this
green and gray terrarium
where cars nose and duck the poles while

paper flies. To spit in the lock of the dark
chained to the meter like a bike
is to wake up dreaming in this light.
Pen scratching the form
of poped release
50 dollars will not fix.
This is what I have.
Cricky neck, creaky track and spine
poured over
and then down.
I touch it; get a little fat
in this air like
dry food puffed with air.
This is what I have:
One lost and savory
pope. One pope aloft.
Two pockets of no light—
self intact. An inventory
of sloppy dust that floats,
that pours in
present tense.

Place of Recovery

I'm practicing my handgun look.
I'm red and angry. A little smaller.
A whole lot denser. I am.
Really. I'm really sorry.

———————————

I come to a decision. I make plans
to purchase things.
I am feeling handsome and genocidal.
"What kills bugs dead!"
I holler.
Here in the hardware store
I am feeling tall and vigorous.
Walking home,
my poison in my bucket.

———————————

I lied. In reality my tummy hurts
which makes me small
and red. And I never leave the house.
How could I have let things get this bad?
I put my head
into my hands. O Lord:
The Place I live in is infested.
Why can I not maintain?
I make a list of things.

———————————

I am writing to tell you
of my recent success.

I am achieving distance
from things.
I stand back
and admire. Take the time
and call it love.
For instance:
I have come here
to the deadbeat café
in order to think of you.
I move my arms
inside my personal space.
Linger delicately
with my fork.
How to say to you
there is moisture inside me?

Today I am feeling talented.
I move my toes.
In order to commune
with my flesh I lie
on the rug. Count
my ribs. Stand up and
face the air.
Somebody help me.

Was that poignant or awkward?
Is this my "good side?"
Do I look, perhaps,
sad? Damp?
Is this good or bad?
Could it be said, perhaps,

that my head is buried
in my enormous and ineffectual
"paws"? Do you think
that I think
that you are watching?

I decide to like myself,
practice my generous look.
(In the mirror: someone. Someone: in the mirror.)
Here, have a drink, I say. Here
have another drink.
I make plans for the future.
In the dark, I remove my hands.
Slowly. Night by Night.
I can feel myself change.

On a night wet with birds
I move my long and friendly arms.
I am growing quiet.
I am growing more quiet.
Like a cigarette in the dark,
my eyes moist and sparkling.
I have many friends
but I am close to no one.
I call it ethics.
It is important. It is almost sexy.
(There are little hairs inside me.)

Valium

In the Kitchen I am called Snowflake
which is to say I'm frilly—
this is some sort of ceremonial dress,
an affection fashioned of florescence.
For the moment nothing exceeds its container.
Because of valium and because of love
there is no end to my gentleness.
All the objects of the world
stand up with their names and are there
no more, no less
totally uninteresting and excellent.

In Praise of Reason

Navigator

1.

I go like this across the surface, mumbling hands
and feet. I trace lines in the surface
mumbling "you," mumbling "here." Everywhere is noise
and also Not Noise and its friend, Little Shapes. I awake suddenly
clutching your hip on the couch. You are asleep
like a rock or like a gulf: a body of water. I am here, sailing, etc.,
and you cannot answer me. Which is why I am standing now
in what is called the dark. Water is pouring from holes drilled
into the belly of the sky and it whacks the pane in whips.
All day I went singing "world" through this liquid.
I came out breathing and hot. Pedaling and pedaling
up the hill of grease to the park in a cloud.
From here the city is gone, digested in fog.
Nothing is left but the infrastructure: trains,
sick canals, trains, power, the trestle in a cloud.
From there the city is also gone. If I could snatch my brain
from its zealous socket, I would take it
and I would irrigate it now.
I would have washed everything
that I could in the world. Your feet, for instance,
with my hands. A year is a terrible place to live
but I write this now to tell you all about these walls,
about this rain, about the pictures where we are.
Everything you already know.

2.

The train is the thing that goes under the ground and
over the ground and the bus is.
And the bus is the thing that goes through us. We ride them.
They are each lessons like the air. We ride them across
the invisible boundaries of political office wanting most to be liked
to our home steeped in booze and love and both varieties of silence.
Pulling back the curtain we reveal the street
empty with things whole and unchanged. And it is a pleasure to be here.
It is a pleasure to be here with you. I know you for one
dishonored in science. Welcome.
To this world of making more bad deals for money.
To this the thrill of our next most excellent mistake.
These walls like walls, these walls are not our friends.
When the landlord invited us here for our race
he began this migration to interior space,
to this room; the foyer of whatever happens next.
Pulling back this curtain I reveal the street
whole with things empty and changed.
And from here the city is also gone.

1/2/00

Here is the train that is locked in ice—

these are sparks—and this
is where the sun comes in

and glides beneath the trees

to the sound of paper falling
in the space between us.

One sound in the intestine of

the invisible dog that is
the odor of myself when blind.

It makes the smell

of horse and burning cars:

transparent non-verbal events
represented now by ( )

equaling
the light that blinds the windows
in the future where I am.

Come sniff that sky

as if it were
behind this sequence of events,
near the place where we are standing,
and was blue.

Real State of the Floating World

I approach the house in tiger pants
thinking of surrender and of holding on.
I see the number but
I can't forget
or remember when I came.
There was light.
The rent was good, the space
intense where
I watched you breathe
in the window room and left and stood
by the outer smoke and birds.
The problem
is wanting to be all Samurai
and dead. I try not to not
want to be profound and slack.
I give a penny to the God of Things.
With fear of haircuts came the spring.
Snow on baby leaves.
D left X then X left Y—
the rent was not reduced.
In a taxi was where I dreamed
of losing shoes, of shoes that swing
from the wires in the world.

Glue Trap

We begin, in a swollen aspect as in prayer,
overlooking some new disease,
spread out like streets
toward a century misplaced in space.
We continue to rise away until
we awake inside
a new mistake and begin to breathe that
bad air. I am so sorry.
I know you did not mean to say that what I said
meant what you said.
So put on your helmet and put on your face.
Might as well put my face against the wall.
(There are mice inside whose job it is to die.)
The apartment rotates, it revolves in rain
and when we awake again it is
to that small and furry kind
of death. Overlooking this we turn away.
I put your hand against the glass.
We touch the surface. Can we call this
a window? I call it
motherfucker or I call it cancer
afraid already of what I've said.
It seems important that they are gray.
Quietly I remove my face.
Next we awake from another dream
about pregnancy and rain,
highway sounds and trees.

The mice still move inside the walls,
they shift and squeak.
Standing on legs we howl.
Our mouths are closed and after that we kiss.
I am forced to understand
that this has become an exorcism, this
perambulation about death.
The most important thing is hair.
One body cracked opens,
a soft and fuzzy egg,
and I take it in my hand, last and
small mistake.

Revelations

I think it might be me who speaks,
head clamped between my knees.
To my face I say: my face. Listen:
To my face I say—
In Two I find a stain and
I press myself against it.
I call it world. (Though I wasn't born to talk
I seem to talk a lot.)
In Three you break my heart
and I stand mute, beseeching.
It's delicious when you return,
I kneel and begin.
In Four I break your heart
and you return to break my face.
This in a motel, under a mountain, in Missoula.
Five is headache where I am now.
I'm sorry I invented you to speak.
I cleaned the kitchen, look.
I bought a yellow clock.
Six is tawdry fantasy.
We kneel and begin to eat.
It's called The Book of Tongues and is
not a prayer to God.
In Eight I'm ravished.
Is it you who speaks in me?
To my face I say: unclench yourself.
(To myself I say: unclench your face.)
The rest is lost in The Lubricious.
Breathing interrupts our lips.

Navigator (Reprise)

Clutching your hip on the couch in its shape
Tracing that shape to its noise
Is a genial logic which allows us to pursue.
(Everywhere else is cups upturned.)
And this is how to listen to the floor.
(I am speaking on the floor.)
I would have washed everything in winter,
I would have tasted anything to taste.
Your shoes, for instance, with my tongue
Is a function in the city.
When we were two against the wall
Everywhere and its friend The Law
Traced this silence to its shape
To this year like Anyplace.
(And from the city we are also gone.)

In Praise of Reason

We made the plan and the plan
is to be happy, it is happiness.

For we have been given remarkable faculties.
(For lord sometimes I can even see.)

We stand in the mirror in our bodies, the bodies we have
and our minds

is a private surface.

If we put helmets on our heads it is in order to protect our brains.

It is OK.

It is like a list and
I am crossing off everything because now I am finished.

•

It is raining in Brooklyn and we are touching the rain
so that we know we are in Brooklyn so we know that we are

home from the recent streets, recently wet.

Someone, someone insane, whispers in the streets when we pass.
Something inaudible, some malediction in the streets when we pass.

There is great potential for what is.

The air is heavy with this potential,
the air splits its seams and is wet

and the result is noise and also distance.

•

Happy as a shape-like tub.

A shape in the tub.

Is a small animal has no name.

Is unidentified when it appears
near the daily furniture.

It is not our pet.

Touch it and we can disappear.

And this is happiness, and its vicinity, regular like rain.

•

I bought the map. I can point
to the map and I can say

"you." I can say "here."
I can say "it is," while I
look inside your body
while I investigate the noise

as this shadow covers the terrain.

I will call this part "In Praise of Reason."
I have thoughts about a blue and quiet god.

•

It's time to go back inside our bodies.

We can sleep here, the weather is right.

All my life, can I say this yet?

I have wanted to be a little older,

a little more dead in the nerves

                    (but not the heart)

and the result is this noise and distance.

FENCEbooks

Zirconia
Chelsey Minnis
WINNER OF THE 2001 ALBERTA PRIZE

Miss America
Catherine Wagner

The Red Bird
Joyelle McSweeney
WINNER OF THE 2002 FENCE MODERN POETS SERIES

Can You Relax in My House
Michael Earl Craig

The Real Moon of Poetry & Other Poems
Tina Brown Celona
WINNER OF THE 2002 ALBERTA PRIZE

Apprehend
Elizabeth Robinson
WINNER OF THE 2003 FENCE MODERN POETS SERIES

Nota
Martin Corless-Smith

FENCE was launched in the spring of 1998. A biannual journal of poetry, fiction, art and criticism, *Fence* has a mission to publish challenging writing and art distinguished by idiosyncrasy and intelligence rather than by allegiance with camps, schools, or cliques. *Fence* has published works by some of the most esteemed contemporary writers as well as excellent work by the completely unknown. It is part of our mission to support young writers who might otherwise have difficulty being recognized because their work doesn't appeal to either the mainstream or to accepted modes of experimentation.

FENCEbooks is an extension of that mission; with our books we hope to provide expanded exposure to poets and writers whose work is excellent, challenging, and truly original. The Alberta Prize is an annual series administered by *Fence Books* in conjunction with the Alberta duPont Bonsal Foundation. The Alberta Prize offers publication of a first or second book of poems by a woman, as well as a $5,000 cash prize.

Our second prize series is the Fence Modern Poets Series, published in cooperation with **saturnalia books**. This contest is open to poets of either gender and at any stage in their career, be it a first book or fifth, and offers a $1,000 cash prize in addition to book publication.

For more information about either prize, visit our website at www.fencebooks.com, or send an SASE to *Fence Books*/[Name of Prize], 14 Fifth Avenue, #1A, New York, NY 10011.

To see more about *Fence*, visit www.fencemag.com

God,
Help Me
Rebuild My
Broken World

MICHAEL YOUSSEF

HARVEST HOUSE PUBLISHERS
EUGENE, OREGON

Cover by Knail, Salem, Oregon

Cover photo © iStockphoto / DNY59

Published in association with Don Gates of the literary agency The Gates Group, www.the-gates-group.com.

GOD, HELP ME REBUILD MY BROKEN WORLD

Copyright © 2016 by Michael Youssef
Published by Harvest House Publishers
Eugene, Oregon 97402
www.harvesthousepublishers.com

ISBN 978-0-7369-5583-6 (pbk.)
ISBN 978-0-7369-5584-3 (eBook)

Library of Congress Cataloging-in-Publication Data

Names: Yousseff, Michael, author.
Title: God, help me rebuild my broken world / Michael Youssef.
Description: Eugene, Oregon: Harvest House Publishers, 2016.
Identifiers: LCCN 2016008063 | ISBN 9780736955836 (pbk.)
Subjects: LCSH: Bible. Nehemiah—Criticism, interpretation, etc.
Classification: LCC BS1365.52.Y68 2016 | DDC 222/.806—dc23 LC record available at https://lccn.loc.gov/2016008063

Printed in the United States of America

16 17 18 19 20 21 22 23 24 / BP-KBD / 10 9 8 7 6 5 4 3 2 1